SUCCESSFUL INTERVIEWING

THE NO NONSENSE LIBRARY

NO NONSENSE CAREER GUIDES

Managing Time
No Nonsense Management
How to Choose a Career
How to Re-enter the Workforce
How to Write a Resume
Successful Interviewing
Succeeding With Difficult People

NO NONSENSE FINANCIAL GUIDES

How to Use Credit and Credit Cards
Investing in Mutual Funds
Investing in the Stock Market
Investing in Tax Free Bonds
Understanding Money Market Funds
Understanding IRA's
Understanding Treasury Bills and Other U.S. Government Securities
Understanding Common Stocks
Understanding Stock Options and Futures Markets
Understanding Social Security
Understanding Insurance
How to Plan and Invest for Your Retirement
Making a Will and Creating Estate Plans
Understanding Condominiums and Co-ops
How to Buy a Home
Understand Mortgages and Home Equity Loans

NO NONSENSE SUCCESS GUIDES

NO NONSENSE HEALTH GUIDES

NO NONSENSE COOKING GUIDES

NO NONSENSE PARENTING GUIDES

NO NONSENSE CAR GUIDES

NO NONSENSE CAREER GUIDE™

SUCCESSFUL
INTERVIEWING

. . . . .

Andrew Ambraziejus

LONGMEADOW
P R E S S

Published by Longmeadow Press, 201 High Ridge Road, Stamford,
CT 06904. All rights reserved. No part of this book may be
reproduced or utilized in any form or by any means, electronic or
mechanical, including photocopying, recording or by any information storage and retrieval system, without permission in writing
from the Publisher. Longmeadow Press and Colophon are trademarks.

Cover design by Nancy Sabato

Interior design by Richard Oriolo

ISBN: 0-681-00565-3

Printed in the United States of America

0 9 8 7 6 5 4 3 2

ACKNOWLEDGMENTS

The author would like to thank Gail Altsher Jasne, Linda Dreyer, Paul Fornario.

C O N T E N T S

. . . . .

Introduction

You are sitting in the reception area, waiting to be called for a job interview with Mr. Jones. You are absentmindedly flipping through a magazine, too nervous to concentrate. The job sounds very good, and you know you are well qualified, but you are worried because you want to make sure you present those qualifications in the best possible light. Many questions are racing through your mind: What will Mr. Jones be like? What will he ask you? Will his questions be simple and straightforward or probing and tricky? What will be the best answers to give him, so you get the job?

Anyone who holds a job has probably been through this scenario. Now compare it to what Mary, another interviewee for the same job, experiences after she arrives in the reception area to wait her turn.

Although she is not one hundred percent sure she has all the qualifications for the job, she has done some research on it and firmly believes that she can quickly pick up the few skills she may be lacking. Like you, she's not totally calm, but she's not suffering from stage fright either. She knows she has prepared herself as best she can for this interview by studying up on the company, going over her qualifications, and making sure she can communicate what she wants to do with her professional life. More than anything, she is curious about Mr. Jones and the job itself. She has a list of questions that she wants to ask him to make sure this job fits in with her future plans. She picks up a magazine and flips through it absentmindedly, eager to meet Mr. Jones and find out more about the job.

Which person seems to be in a better frame of mind in this situation? Most people would say that Mary's confidence increases her likelihood of getting the job. But there's something else. If you look closely, you will see that Mary is more concerned with finding out about the job rather than focusing her energies on worrying about how she will come across in the interview. She seems to have discovered the secret to good interviewing: She is an equal partner in the interview process. While aware that she will probably do more of the talking during the interview, and Mr. Jones will do more of the listening, which is the nature of the interview process, she has her share of questions as well. And she believes she has a right to ask these questions. She wants to know that the job fits her needs as much as she wants to convince Mr. Jones that she fits the needs of the job.

The purpose of this book is to get you to look at interviewing in the same way as Mary. Take an active role in the entire process. Think of yourself as an equal partner who has some power in this situation too. Tell yourself that you are trying to find the right job; the job is not out to find you.

There will be many benefits to successful interviewing. Very importantly, you will be more relaxed during the interview itself. You will focus on the job and the interviewer, and you won't have time to worry about yourself. You will also naturally come across as more confident, and your interest in the job will show through very clearly—qualities that all interviewers are looking for. The very act of asking questions will impress the interviewer as well—no one wants to hire people who don't seem interested in what they will be doing eight hours a day, five days a week.

Most managers agree that an interview is the single most important factor in your being hired for the job. So use it to your advantage. Instead of merely being a passive participant, hoping you will be chosen, take an active role. Understand that you are there to choose as well. Paradoxically, you will discover that the more you think about the job and stop worrying about yourself, the better you will come across to your interviewer.

O N E

. . . . .

Preparation: Putting a Support System Together

Taking an active role in the interview process means being well prepared. And that in itself is a process. Interviews don't just happen. There are many steps leading up to an interview. And whether you are aware of it or not, the choices you make at each of these steps will influence the final outcome. Think of this part of the process as creating a support system for yourself. You are laying the groundwork so that during the interview everything will flow smoothly, and you can worry about the specifics of the job instead of yourself.

Preparation includes a whole range of activities that you are responsible for: getting together your resume, preparing cover letters, lining up references, doing research on the firm and position you desire. Done well, these will all come together at the moment that counts and help present you in the best possible light to the interviewer.

Your first task is to do an inventory of yourself—your short-term and long-term goals, job expectations, skills, accomplishments, possible flaws that need to be addressed. After all, you will be interviewing for a job that *you* want. You have to be totally clear on why you want it. The interviewer will want to know that, and a few other things as well. Can you handle the job? Do your goals match the company's? Will you fit in with other employees? Because you will be asked different types of questions along these lines, you want to be sure you can respond to them without hesitation.

Even if you think you know the answers to all such questions, do not skimp on your preparation. You will find that there is a huge difference between having what you want to say somewhere in the back of your mind and being ready to explain a point in a brief, clear way. When every moment counts, as it does in an interview, the difference of even a few seconds can be crucial.

Your Self-Inventory

To begin your self-inventory, sit down with pencil and paper in a quiet place and devote a few hours to thinking about yourself in terms of your profession. Where are you at this point in your life? Are you just going for your first job, or are you trying to make the big jump into a management position—or into a new career altogether?

Think of the future—one year, two years, ten years down the road. Where do you want to be in terms of work? Jot down all the positive and negative aspects of anything you come up with. And if you have no clear idea of where you want to be, admit this also. Being realistic is important. At this point, you have nothing to gain and much to lose by glossing over problems, weaknesses, or goals that you are unsure of.

As you sit there, trying to sort it all out, imagine yourself in the interview being asked the following two things:

- Tell me about yourself.
- What are you looking for?

Essentially, that is what the interviewer is going to want to know about you. The first question focuses on your qualifications, and the second focuses on the job you want. Of course, these two queries are so broad, you could spend hours discussing them. You won't be doing that in the interview—so do it now. Since you're under no pressure, you can give yourself a chance to think through the long-term. As you see, from the very beginning, you start taking control, picking and choosing what you will want to emphasize during your job search. This is why preparation is so important.

As you go through this all-important first step, remember that there are no "right" answers. In fact, there are no answers at all. First of all, what's right for you is not necessarily right for someone else. Also, jobs and interviewers differ from each other. You may interview with two people for one particular job, and they may

3

each react differently to you or emphasize different aspects of the job. You can't predict any of this. Rather than formulating specific, canned answers to possible questions, think of topics and areas of concern that you feel are important. The only thing that will be a constant, the one thing that all your interviewers will be impressed by, is if they see that you know your own mind. Self-knowledge will always be more important than any specific answer because it will give you the flexibility to respond intelligently to anything that may come up. And nothing will turn an interviewer off faster than hearing an answer that sounds rehearsed.

Remember, too, that at this point you are not thinking only about a job interview. The answers you come up with in your self-inventory will determine the kinds of jobs you try for, what you put on your resume, how you word your cover letter, how you "coach" your references—in fact, the direction your entire job-search process takes. So work through the following points carefully, and for best effect, do this over a period of a few days. By going back over your notes you will see what you missed the first time and can gauge how honest and realistic your self-inventory really is.

- What are your goals? Know what you want to say when asked this question or anything similar, both about the short- and the long-term. This does not mean that your life is totally mapped out, but it does mean that you have thought about what you want to do based on your abilities, desires, and monetary concerns. This shows an interviewer that you care enough about yourself to focus on the future.

A lot of people, especially those just getting out of school, are confused about what they want to do and would throw up their hands if asked to define their goals. There is nothing wrong with this but, unfortunately, it doesn't help in getting a job. If you don't know how to answer this basic question, first try to determine why you feel this way. Perhaps there are things that you would like to do, but for some reason, feel that you shouldn't. Perhaps you like a lot of things and just can't seem to choose. Or perhaps this confusion hides deeper fears, like an overall sense of insecurity. Don't be afraid to talk to someone whom you trust about this confusion—chances are, they've been there, too. Asking a personal friend or relative, or a guidance counselor at school is a good way to start. For those out of school, there are professional organizations to turn to: mental health clinics that deal with job problems, job placement offices, career counseling organizations. And remember that your local library is also a good source of information—it will not only have books and magazines on related topics but may even have job placement services as well.

- What are your strengths/weaknesses? Although the tendency among interviewers today is to ask questions in a less direct, more open-ended way, this old standby is still a good question to review. Think about it both in personal and professional terms. Remember, even if this question is not phrased exactly this way, the interviewer will want to know where you shine and where you don't.

- Do an inventory of your accomplishments and contributions in previous jobs. Think of tasks you did or changes you made that you are most proud of. Have specific figures or data to back yourself up. For example: If you increased sales, by what percentage? If you changed the way a certain job was done, how was it done before. What were the benefits to your company and co-workers? If you're just starting out, think of school or community activities or even hobbies that gave you a sense of satisfaction. However, always be careful of puffing yourself up. Make sure you are honest about the extent of the responsibility you are claiming. If under more careful questioning the interviewer discovers that you were only part of a group effort or were forced into doing something by circumstances beyond your control, it will not reflect well on you.

- What are your skills? First, think in terms of specific jobs you can do and machines you can operate. Then, think of your "people" skills: managing, organizing, designing systems, motivating co-workers.

- Do you have any role models or mentors? This is always a good thing to think about because it indirectly says a lot about your attitudes and goals. It is a good way of telling an interviewer a lot about yourself in a few words. Just be careful to have good, sincere reasons for your choice: picking a currently famous personality or a tried-and-true figure from history will only sound obvious and facile.

- What is your philosophy of life? How do you define success? How important is money to you? What would or wouldn't you sacrifice for a promotion at work? Being able to articulate your value system will serve you well with many managers. How you answer a question like that will indicate to them how successfully you will fit into their organization. So think this through carefully.
- Evaluate your current job. Why do you want to leave it? What have you learned from it? What do you like and what don't you like about it? How much have you grown since you began that job?
- Go over any negatives. There may be negative aspects to your current job (such as a personality conflict with your supervisor) or in your work history (such as a gap in time when you did not work). Now is the time to pinpoint these problem areas and determine how you will deal with them should they come up in interviews.
- Think about your ideal working environment. The job you are interviewing for may not have perfect working conditions. Will that be okay with you? How far will you deviate from your ideal? What will you tell the interviewer? Things to think about are noise and stress levels, offices versus cubicles, group versus individual projects, the lack of certain equipment that you were used to in a previous job.
- Why are you choosing this particular job, company, industry? This question will come up in various forms at every interview. Have good reasons that don't contradict anything else you've said.

The need to be consistent in what you tell your interviewer is another reason why thorough preparation is necessary. The minute you contradict yourself and start backtracking or explaining something a second time, you have raised doubts in the interviewer's mind about your honesty or your commitment. And you have probably lost your chance for the job.

The line between canned answers and quick, clear responses is a fine one, but it does exist. The more thorough your self-inventory, the better you will be able to answer any unexpected questions and sound honest and unrehearsed while doing so.

The Resume

An amusing story about resumes recently made the rounds of personnel offices in New York City. It concerned a young man who worked at a men's toiletries counter in a large department store. Wanting a new job, he asked a friend to type up his resume and gave this friend specific instructions on what to capitalize, where to start new paragraphs, how many tab spaces to indent. At an interview, which was going along just fine, he was taken aback when the interviewer pointed to his resume and asked what the letters TABS next to the department store name meant. It was at that moment that the young man realized his friend had typed out what had merely been an instruction to indent a particular line. In a panic, trying to decide whether to admit that he had not proofread his resume carefully enough, the young man suddenly came out with, "Oh, TABS. That's Toning, Aftershave, Body Shop—the name of my department at the store." The rest of the interview went on as before, and he got the new job.

The moral of the story? Either be able to think very quickly on your feet or proofread your resume and then proofread it again! Although it seems minor, a small mistake like that can sour the whole interview, giving the person behind the desk the impression that you are sloppy or that you don't really care enough about getting the job.

Although we don't know what would have happened had the young man admitted his mistake, this anecdote highlights a problem that you will face in the entire job-search process and in composing your resume, in particular: Every little bit counts. There is much competition for every desirable job, and every applicant has precious little time in which to impress the interviewer. Think about it. If a manager or personnel officer has to go through twenty, thirty, a hundred resumes for a particular job listing, each resume gets only a quick glance of perhaps a minute, if that. A manager needs to digest the information quickly.

So think of your resume as your selling tool. It has to do its job in the shortest amount of time possible, providing a quick reference to your past and highlighting certain areas that you want the interviewer to focus on. With this in mind, you can understand how both *what* you put down and *how* you put it down matters.

The look of your resume.
"I want it snappy, short, and easy to look at."

"I don't read it unless I can pick things out immediately."
"If it looks too fancy, I don't trust it."

The above are typical comments made by personnel officers and employment counselors who read resumes day in and day out. As you can see, the look of a resume matters greatly. With so much to read, they don't want to spend time hunting for pertinent information—it's your job to make it easy to find. The look and feel of the resume is important because it is the first thing a person notices when taking the resume out of the envelope. Whether consciously or unconsciously, he is looking for an overall feeling of clarity, responding to the color of the paper and its texture, the neatness and layout of the page, and, the readability of the typeface.

You want your resume to pull this person in, make him want to read it more closely instead of giving him an immediate reason to reject you. In preparing your resume, keep the following things in mind:

- Use 8½ x 11-inch size paper.
- Stay away from flimsy copier paper. Nice bond paper (20-24 lb. weight) is perfectly acceptable. You do not have to get fancy and use expensive, heavier paper, especially if you're just starting out. If you do, it may be seen as extravagant.
- Follow a similar rule-of-thumb in regard to a professionally printed resume. You do not need to go through the expense of having it done, certainly not if it's your first or second job. The taboo against having a resume photocopied is gone—though of course you want to use decent paper and make sure that the copy machine gives clean, crisp reproductions.

- If you use a home computer for your resume, make sure it's printed on a laser or letter-quality printer (dot matrix is not acceptable).
- White and light off-white paper (cream, ivory, light gray) are good choices. Stay away from anything flashier unless you are applying for an artistic or designrelated position where bright colors are more accepted.
- One or two pages is fine. Try for one page, especially if you are at the beginning stages of your career, but no one is going to hold it against you if your resume has concrete, pertinent information and spills over onto a second page.
- Use bullets to highlight information.
- Proofread, proofread, proofread—and have others proofread your resume, too! Remember, small details matter.

In designing your resume, think of it as different blocks of information: one layout and spacing for dates, another for titles, another for job descriptions. The purpose of separating these different blocks of information with white space and giving each a particular look (all in capital letters, underlined, etc.) is so that a person immediately knows what he is looking at. The individual design is up to you; simplicity and clarity are your main concerns.

You will also have to decide between using a chronological or a functional layout for your resume. The chronological layout essentially follows the timetable of your career—you list your last job first and go backward from there. This format is the one most commonly used. Not only are those who may be hiring you interested in what you did most recently, but looking at how you progressed in your career over time is a good, quick way to acquaint them with your professional accomplishments.

A functional resume lists your experience by the kinds of work you have done. People use this format if they have different areas of expertise that they want to give equal weight to. It is also a way to minimize time gaps in your resume. A functional resume's primary drawback is that it can be hard to read and may even cause the person going over it to search for inconsistencies.

The content of your resume. There is much disagreement these days about what was once a staple of all resumes—your job objective. Many managers and employment counselors feel that having a job objective listed on your resume hurts rather than helps. Unless you are absolutely sure you want a particular kind of job, it can easily box you in and give people one other reason to reject you. Some feel, however, that having a job objective shows that you have thought things through carefully and know where you want to go with your professional life. Ultimately, this question is for you to decide. As a general rule of thumb, if you are open to a number of possibilities or are just starting out, leave off the job objective.

Leaving a job objective off the actual resume, however, doesn't mean you don't need to keep one in mind as you are putting your resume together. Having a mental job objective will help you focus and decide what information to put down and how to word it. By doing this, every entry of your resume will implicitly point toward what you want to do next.

In deciding what to put on your resume, keep in mind the following:

- Use specifics: exact job titles, the number of people you assisted or supervised, who you reported to, specific duties.
- Use verbs: "increased sales," "managed a department," "ran meetings," "conducted research." Verbs are active, not passive, and show that you were in charge. Of course, don't claim that you were responsible for something you weren't; don't say you ran meetings if you only participated in them.
- Include contributions and accomplishments. Go back to your self-inventory and pick out the most important ones for each job.
- List particular skills. Specifics are especially important here. Avoid broad generalizations like "work well coordinating projects." Instead list the projects you coordinated, and during the interview itself, tell how well you did the job.
- List your name, address, and phone number at top of your resume (on both pages if it runs to two). Whether this block of information is centered or in the upper right corner or somewhere else depends on your overall design—your main concern is that it's immediately noticeable.

Some things you should NOT put on your resume:

- Never list references.
- Don't put down personal information (height, weight, marital status, children).
- Don't use adjectives or adverbs. Don't say it was a

"complex" project or a "large" department—give the number of people involved in the project or working in the department. Again, a resume is not the place to say how well you did something—you don't have the space to waste. Save such descriptions for the interview.

- Avoid jargon. This is especially true if you are changing fields or careers. Remember, your main objective is to communicate, clearly and quickly. Use language that will be familiar to whoever is reading your resume. While there may be some job titles and specific duties that will need explanation, using too many of these will seem like puffery.

Finally, remember that periodically you will have to update your resume. If you just add on to it, your resume will start looking padded and unfocused. As you change jobs, gain responsibilities, and learn new skills, you will want to add these to your resume and prune out those things that are no longer relevant or that you have outgrown. For example, if you used to type letters and now have been promoted to copywriting, which includes typing skills, you can drop any reference to typing because it is understood as a component of copywriting, which carries greater responsibility.

The Cover Letter

With few exceptions, a cover letter should accompany every resume you send out—whether it's in response to a newspaper advertisement, a referral, or just a blind stab in the dark.

However, a cover letter is not just a formality; it serves the purpose of introducing you to your potential employer. Your resume has the facts, figures, and specifics. While your cover letter should be succinct as well, it should also be a little more personal. It is your opportunity to highlight one or two facts from your resume and to state your reasons for applying for a particular job.

A cover letter is especially useful when you are changing careers and you feel a bit of explanation is in order. This letter is an excellent way of stating your reasons for your career change and for setting an agenda for the interview that may follow. It also serves as a useful calling card if you have been referred to a particular job by a third party and want to say how you found out about the opening.

The tone of your cover letter should be professional, but not dry. That is, you want it to be friendly, upbeat, and informative, and not cutesy, sloppy, or difficult to understand in any way. You want a tone that conveys enthusiasm and the sense that you can add much to the organization that is receiving your resume. All this, of course, has to be done in a few sentences. The people who have to go through all those resumes also have to read all those cover letters. Brevity assures that your letter is really read.

In composing your cover letter use the first sentence to introduce yourself. If you are answering an ad in the paper, refer to the specific ad and the position being advertised, and mention the name of the paper and the date as well. If you have been referred by someone, give the particulars. Your next two or three sentences are the body of the letter. Here you highlight a few important facts from your resume, state why you want the job, and why you would be good at it. Your enthusiasm and willingness to work hard should be implicit in these statements. In your last sentence, state your hope that you will be called for an interview. If the letter is being sent to a particular person, say that you will call at some specific time in the near future to see if you can arrange a meeting.

Use the same kind of stationery as you do for your resume, but as opposed to the resume, do not use bullets or underlining or other fancy design elements. A letter is meant to be read, not examined. In the cover letter it is the words that get your message across, not their look.

References

The important thing to remember about your references is to line them up *before* you have your interview. It is not only courteous to the people who will be giving you a good word, but it also prepares them for the call so that they will have time to organize their thoughts.

When you know that you will be having an interview, call up the people you want to give as references and ask if it is all right for you to do so. Tell them what you know about the company and the position you are interviewing for. This information will not only help them sort out their own thoughts, but they may offer some insights and advice that you can use on your interview.

Your interviewer will want professional, not personal, references. As an employment counselor put it, "Even Hitler could have gotten personal references. I don't trust them." Ideally, you will have two or three professional references—previous bosses are the most desirable. If you are looking for your first job, line up professors and guidance counselors from school. References from anyone who worked with you in volunteer or community organizations will also be helpful.

Whenever you leave a job, try to get your boss to give you a reference in writing. Having a piece of paper that you can take with you to any future interview will not only look impressive but will save you time in tracking down old bosses and rekindling their enthusiasm for you.

Giving your references information about the job and the company you will be interviewing for allows you to go over some pertinent facts and even do some coaching. Tell your reference how you will be presenting yourself in the interview, what aspects of your experience you will be emphasizing, and which of your skills you think the new job will be utilizing.

How well your references do their job, of course, will depend on their conversation with whoever calls them. Here are additional pointers to give them to achieve maximum effectiveness:

- Whoever calls will be looking for some *punch*. Most people can get decent references. A good interviewer can read between the lines and will only be impressed with real enthusiasm and conviction.
- If someone is given a positive reference, a tactic that one veteran interviewer uses is to ask, "What is the *worst* thing that you can say about X?" This question often catches people off guard and can elicit hesitation or a truth that you may not be happy

about. So cover all your bases and prepare your references for this possibility.

Research

Research is fundamental. Every interviewer will be impressed if you know the basics about the company or industry you are hoping to work in. Conversely, they will all look unfavorably at that passive shrug of the shoulders or shake of the head when you reveal that you know very little.

Doing research before an interview will benefit you in the following ways. It will

- show the interviewer that you are motivated
- allow you to ask more pointed and well-thought out questions
- help you focus more on the job rather than yourself and your nervousness
- help you make better decisions about the job you take, the salary you accept, and the responsibilities you agree to take on

Any amount of research will give you more control of the whole interviewing process. At the very least, you should know what the company produces or what services it provides. Also, try to get a sense of how big the company is and where it is positioned in the industry. If you can, learn about its profitability. See if you can find out about any industry trends. Be aware of the company's products—whether they're cars, books, or furniture—and any awards that these products might have won.

Know the company logo. And last, but never least, know how to pronounce the company name and how to spell it! This is often overlooked, yet it is crucial; imagine how you would feel if someone wanted to work for you and mispronounced your name during the interview.

The more of these facts you have at your fingertips, the better you will be able to discuss the potential job and your expectations of it. Be careful, however, that you don't fall into the trap of showing off your knowledge—that will be a definite turnoff for the interviewer. For example, if you are applying for an entry-level position as a secretary and launch into a discussion of the company's profitability over the last ten years, you are going overboard. While you want to express some knowledge of the company, take your cues from the interview itself. If the interviewer happens to ask you about profitability and you happen to know something about it, that's wonderful. But don't volunteer information just for the sake of scoring points.

The library is your main source of information. There are a number of books available that describe the firms in various industries, list their personnel, give each company's approximate size, and describe their products and services. Ask the librarian for help in finding information on the particular industry you are interested in.

Besides the library's reference materials, you can also use the following:

- Newspapers and general-interest magazines, available either in the library or at your newsstand. They are especially useful for current news on industry trends, particular awards, certain problems in the field.

- "Trade" magazines. Each industry usually has its own magazine. Become familiar with it.
- Anyone who works in the industry or, better yet, in the company where the interview is scheduled. If you know someone who knows someone who works in the same industry, don't be afraid of trying to arrange a meeting. An "insider" can quickly point you in the right direction.
- A corporate newsletter. If you can get your hands on one quickly, it will give you the tone and feel of the place. If you are afraid to contact the company yourself, see if you can have a friend call up for you. Usually, such newsletters are produced by the public relations (or publicity or corporate communications) departments.

TWO

·····

Clothes: Conveying Style and Professionalism

Here are some comments from personnel recruiters about how to dress for an interview:

> *"Don't try to prove how much of an individual you are with your clothes. Prove it with your answers."*
>
> *"I like a little flair."*
>
> *"I react negatively when a person doesn't look totally put together."*
>
> *"It's the details that matter."*
>
> *"I wouldn't presume to tell you what to wear, but I'll notice immediately if it doesn't look right."*
>
> *"All I know is that you can't look like Cher—until you get the job!"*

These comments illustrate what you are faced with when selecting clothes for an interview: No one is going to tell you what to wear, but everyone will have an opinion about it when it seems wrong. Looking right entails presenting yourself in both a flattering and professional manner. While you want to look stylish, you also want to convey a sense of responsibility, the impression that not only will you take your job seriously but that you will do it well at all times.

The trick lies in successfully integrating both your own sense of style and the required professional look. Some general guidelines to remember:

- Choose natural fibers over synthetics.
- Wool is more of a professional look than cotton.
- Wear a suit; it carries the most authority.
- For a nonmanagement position, blazers and pants are acceptable for men.
- Professional-type dresses are acceptable for women.
- Avoid bright, primary colors.
- Avoid loud patterns and plaids.
- It's better to be bland than outlandish.
- You can't go wrong with a traditional, conservative look.
- Sloppiness virtually guarantees rejection.

When you are deciding on what to wear, consider the industry you want to join. Banking and other financial institutions tend to require very conservative dress; communications industries, such as advertising and publishing, are less conservative, while retail, sales, or other high-visibility jobs require a very stylish, polished look. If you are interviewing for a job as a teacher, looking too stylish might cost you the job; accessibility and friendliness are more important than trend setting fashions or a corporate look.

Also, consider the position you are interviewing for. You don't want to be more authoritatively dressed than your prospective boss. If this is your first job and you come in wearing a suit that costs five hundred dollars, you could easily appear to be flaunting your wealth or status. At the same time, don't "dress down" unless you are interviewing for a job in a very informal work environment, such as an artist's studio.

Use accessories to express style and individuality. For women, that can mean a nice scarf or an interesting lapel pin or other jewelry (as long as it's not too gaudy or distracting). Men have a little less leeway; their primary choices lie in the pattern and color of their ties, as well their suits or blazers. No single element should stand out; everything should blend into one sharp, polished look that implies effectiveness and efficiency.

And watch those details. Scuffed shoes with worn heels are a frequent complaint. Women shouldn't carry oversized handbags and should stay away from bright-red nail polish or heavily scented perfume. Tight or ill-filling clothes should also be avoided. If money is an important consideration, buy one good suit rather than two mediocre ones—you can use accessories to dress it up. Good grooming, of course, is a given—especially of the hands, which are often neglected. And plan ahead of time to make sure that what you wear is adequately pressed and cleaned.

Above all, think of your interview wardrobe as something that will produce a feeling of security in your interviewer: security that you are reliable, that you take your responsibilities seriously, that you will fit in well with the organization. A certain style and pizzazz are most welcome, but not at the cost of alienating the person who will be your boss.

T H R E E

·····

Getting the Interview: Answering Want Ads and Gathering Information

While you are getting your "support system" together and polishing your interview look, you are also conducting your actual job search.

When most of us talk about searching for work, we are usually referring to looking through the classified section of the newspaper, noting any position that sounds interesting or that utilizes the particular skills we have. When we have found those positions, we send our resume and cover letter to the address listed and wait for a response.

While there is nothing wrong with this approach, you should realize that it is essentially a passive way of going about a job search. In addition, it is estimated that newspaper ads cover only about 20 to 25 percent of the actual jobs that are available at any given time. Therefore if you use only this one method, you are spending 100 percent of your time on 20 to 25 percent of what is really available, leaving the other 75 to 80 percent of the market untapped.

This untapped market is usually referred to as the "hidden" job market because it consists of positions that are not advertised in the newspaper. The people who land those jobs are referred by friends and acquaintances, find out about existing jobs through professional contacts, are promoted from within the same company when a job becomes available, or have positions created for them because they have unique qualifications in a certain field. You, too, can tap into this market by

- Sending out your resume to a number of firms in a particular industry and asking for work based on your qualifications
- Networking and participating in informational interviews

While getting a job is possible by blindly sending out your resumes, it is very much a stab in the dark. For every hundred resumes you send out, you will get a couple of responses—not a very good batting average. In addition, getting all that paperwork together and sending out all those resumes is both time consuming and costly. To better that ratio, try to find out whatever you can about the various companies and industries you are interested in: who has been doing a lot of hiring and firing, which is a growth industry and what are the up-and-coming firms within that industry, which ones are on the lookout for particular skills you have—the more noteworthy the better. Do some extra research in the library. Read those trade publications. The more reasons you have for sending your resume to a particular firm, the more intelligently you can present yourself, thereby increasing the possibility that you will be called for an interview.

A far better way to increase your chances of landing job interviews is by conducting what are known as "informational" interviews, which are really a form of networking. In these, you are taking an active approach to the interview process and maybe even creating some job openings for yourself.

The informational interview is helpful when you are starting out and looking for your first job in a particular industry. By talking to people already working within the industry you will get knowledgeable answers without any hype. This is also a good tactic to use when you are changing careers. Because you won't know very many people in your new field, conducting informational interviews will help you build contacts as well as gather information. Look at it as an investment in the future.

The most important thing to remember is that an informational interview is for information only—it is not conducted with the hope of landing a specific job. The interviewer has graciously granted you time to answer some questions and point you in the right direction on your career search. Look at it as a favor, which it often is. Take your cue from the person behind the desk—if she brings up the possibility of working for the company or trying for a specific job, so much the better. *Then* you can begin to discuss the job itself.

Before setting up an informational interview, think about all your professional and personal acquaintances who are working in that particular field. Talk to them, but don't forget about those who may be only tangentially involved in a certain area. They may not be able to give you very much information, but they may give you a referral.

Aside from personally knowing somebody who works in an industry, getting interviews through referrals is the best way to make contacts. Because such interviews are usually granted as favors for mutual acquaintances, the people you see will generally be accommodating and will go out of their way to give you the best information they can. The mutual acquaintance referral is also a very good way of actually building a network. Once you have finished talking to person A, hopefully you will be given the name of person B, who will refer you to person C, and so on. Your network begins to grow. The drawback to this whole process is that it tends to take time. Everyone has her own schedule, and you will usually have to wait before you can set up the next meeting. That is why you must look at it as an investment in the future; all this information may not pay off immediately, but it will help you down the road.

Another advantage of building a network is that you will get better at it with each successive interview. You will pick up knowledge from one person that you can use in formulating questions for the next person you see. After a while, almost without realizing it, you will have gathered quite a bit of information. As you use this information to sharpen your own questions, you will begin to impress the people who see you. Your chances for job offers will increase, and you will be in a better position to make intelligent decisions about any job you are trying to get.

If you don't know anyone who can be your person A, it will be research time at the library. Go through the trade magazines and publications on the industry you are interested in, then write letters to the people listed. Department heads are your best bet; presidents and other high-level executives are less likely to answer you. While your chances of getting a response from a blind mailing are not as high as they would be if you were referred by someone, you still may manage to get some interviews.

The trick to setting up meetings in this way lies in getting people's attention with your introductory letter. Keep this letter short; make it as original and honest as you can; and do not enclose your resume. Remember, this is not a search for a specific job; this is an effort to get people to make their time available to you. Also remember that in this case, you are not trying to impress people with your qualifications; you are trying to impress them with your interest in their field. Tell them why; maybe there is something in your past that sparked your interest in that field. You may find that you have something in common with certain people you are writing to. If you become aware of such information, include it in your letter.

If the person getting your letter finds it interesting, amusing, or touching, the better are your chances of a positive response. At the end of each letter, tell the person you will be contacting her by phone to try and set up an interview. If you do get to talk to her and she says she is very busy, suggest an appointment in the future.

And don't forget your school when looking for referrals. Remember that many schools have built up their own network of graduates working in various fields who have volunteered to make themselves available to any students or alumni wanting to talk to them. Use their knowledge.

When you get an interview, plan on its running about a half hour. If it runs ten or fifteen minutes longer, that's a good sign—you had much to discuss and your interviewee was willing to give you the time. If you are approaching an hour, think about ending the interview; you don't want to overstay your welcome.

Remember that you are the one running the show in this instance; you will be asking the questions, so be well prepared. If you feel it is helpful, it is certainly okay during the interview, to refer to a notebook with your questions in it and to write down the information.

When drawing up your list of questions to ask in an informational interview, keep in mind the following topics:

- Education. What kind and how much? Any particular classes or subjects that one should take?
- Skills. What machines should one know how to operate? Computer software? Verbal or mathematical skills? Management skills?
- Promotions. How does one get promoted in the industry? What kinds of jobs lead to the job you are

ultimately interested in? How long would all this take to happen?

- Salaries. What is the pay scale? How long does it take to reach certain levels?
- Personality. Which kinds of personality traits are necessary for success? Which traits are hindrances? Who do the people you are interviewing like to have working for them?
- Typical days. Ask the person to describe a typical day. Focus on the problems that are normally encountered and solved. Ask for a rundown of typical duties also.
- Trends. What is happening in the industry? What are the positive and negative aspects? Where does the person think the industry will be ten years from now?
- Your own background. Toward the end of the interview, give the person you are interviewing your resume to get some feedback. What does the person think you should do to improve your chances of getting work? Which strengths should you build on? Which gaps should you fill?

After you complete your give-and-take, you have one more question to ask: Is there anyone your interviewee can recommend for you to see next? Chances are this person knows a lot of people in the industry, and if you have had a nice, friendly interview, she will be happy to steer you to someone else. She may even make a call or two for you, and you have yourself another referral.

At the end of the interview, thank the person for her time and inquire about leaving extra copies of your resume. If yes, leave two or three. If not, accept this without any to-do. You have just gained much valuable information and have made one (and possibly more) contact for the future.

F O U R

· · · · ·

The Types
of Interviews:
Know What to Expect

Although the most common type of interview is a formal job interview—you meet with your prospective boss to talk about the job and yourself—there are a number of other kinds of interviews you may encounter in your search for work. Each of these interviews differs from the first in a number of important ways.

The Screening Interview

Often, you will go through a screening interview before the formal "selection," "hiring," or "placement" interview takes place. The screening interview is conducted by someone in the personnel or human resources department of a company. Most often, screening interviews take place when you are interviewing for jobs with corporations or large companies that have the money to maintain well-staffed personnel departments. When you interview at a smaller company, many times there is no screening interview or it is performed by the manager, who will also conduct the formal interview.

Because a screening interview is conducted by the personnel department, and because it occurs before the meeting with the manager to whom the position reports, many people regard a screening interview as a mere formality where a few basics are taken care of before the "real" interview. Nothing could be further from the truth. A screening interview, while not the same as a formal interview, still carries a lot of weight.

Take screening interviews seriously! The personnel department has authority—a lot of authority. "If they don't like the color of your shirt, you won't get past them," is the way one executive describes it. The duty of the personnel staff in the screening interview is just what it sounds: stopping unacceptable candidates from going any further in the interview process. If they think something is not right, you will not get to the formal interview stage at all.

That is why your attitude in screening interviews is so important. Respect the personnel department's authority. But this doesn't mean you should be afraid of anyone. Confident, straightforward, and succinct: this best describes how you should present yourself.

Be very wary of pulling rank during a screening

interview by discussing someone you know at the company, as if this acquaintance provides you with some kind of special front-running status. Personnel people are often very sensitive to this ploy. They have a screening job to do, and it doesn't matter how good a friend you are to the daughter of the company's president or to the sales manager. If you feel that your connections in the company can help you during the screening, have them go to personnel and put in a good word for you. A recommendation coming from them will sound more believable than if you beat your own drum.

In assessing candidates, the screening interviewer focuses on facts and figures; the reasons why someone should not be sent on for further interviewing. Can you verify the dates and positions on your resume? Do you have any time gaps in it? Do you have the experience and education the position requires? The skills? Are your references verifiable? Your salary? The last thing a screening interviewer wants is to send a candidate on to meet a prospective boss and then have this boss call later on, complaining that the candidate did not meet the basic requirements of the job. If this happens, it means that personnel is not doing its job, which is to take care of the basics so the manager does not have to waste time going over them.

Because they concentrate on the basics, your personality is not very important to screening interviewers. Save your enthusiasm for the selection interview. In a screening interview, facts are important. Don't volunteer information that has not been asked for. Be prepared to verify everything on your resume. And don't try to impress anyone.

Generally, in a screening interview, you will not be asking many questions yourself. However, be prepared with some questions in case they are solicited by the interviewer. General questions about the company and its organization are perfectly acceptable. (Save the more specific questions about the job for your selection interview.) If your screening interviewer hasn't mentioned company benefits, you can ask about them as part of your questions about the company. Your interviewer may give you a broad outline of benefits and make it understood that any further discussion depends on how well the formal interview goes. This is normal operating procedure. If you are interviewing for a higher-level position, you may have to come back to personnel for a separate interview to discuss these issues.

If your resume is in good order and you are not making any false claims, your screening interview should go very smoothly. Depending on the position and the company, you will either go right on to interview with your prospective boss or you will have to schedule it for a future date. The interviewer will tell you what the next step is in the process.

The Stress Interview

Your formal job interview may turn into a "stress" interview. The following anecdote illustrates what may happen.

Like most interviewees, Mary walked into Mr. Smith's office feeling a little nervous, but at the same hopeful that she would have a good interview with him. She wanted a job as Mr. Smith's assistant and had prepared well by getting a good resume together, learning about the advertising company where Mr. Smith was an account executive, and asking the personnel department during her screening interview a few good questions about the role of the company in the industry.

The interview started well. Mr. Smith asked her some standard questions about her life and professional hopes, and seemed to nod approvingly at everything she said. But then he turned sullen, even curt. Mary didn't know whether it was her imagination or an accurate perception, but every answer she gave in the second half of the interview appeared to be brushed aside with what almost seemed like contempt. Her confidence disappeared, and her answers grew more and more confused because she found it almost impossible to concentrate. She was close to tears when Mr. Smith suddenly started smiling again and ended the interview with a warm handshake and a remark that she was high on his list to come back for a second interview. Mary left in a daze, not knowing whether she would even want to come back a second time to suffer through another humiliating session.

Although most interviewers appreciate how nerve-wracking an interview can be and try to put everyone they see at ease, experiences such as Mary's are not all that uncommon. For some interviewers, stress is part of the game plan, especially if the position being filled will entail a lot of stress. They will give all sorts of unwelcome responses during the interview just to see how the unsuspecting interviewee will react. Others may just be having a bad day because of problems totally unrelated to the interview, and so are in no mood to be friendly. Still others may switch from hot to cold, depending on how successful they are at dealing with their emotions. Whether intentional or not, such reactions from the interviewer do make it very hard to present yourself in a confident, enthusiastic manner, and you can get rattled very easily.

Your best defense against an interviewer's unsupportive attitude is NOT to take it personally. Understand that while there are many possible explanations for the reaction you are getting, the *least* likely one is that it indicates how well your interview is going. Unless you have been unfortunate enough to run into Attila the Hun, most interviewers will not want to show you that you are unfit for a job. So if you suddenly feel that the interview is turning negative or that something else strange is happening, don't let it get you down. See it as a test and prepare to show your mettle. After all, what do you have to lose?

If stress is part of the game plan, one of the most common ways of introducing it into the interview is for the interviewer to be silent: You give an answer to a question, and the interviewer stares at you for what seems like eternity. You become self-conscious and start rambling, adding on to your answer in order to improve it. *Don't*—no matter how many better answers you can think of in the next few seconds. Try to meet your interviewer's silence with your own. If you absolutely can't, ask a question ("Were you looking for more information?") or give a follow-up statement ("I trust that answers your question") What you want to do is give the burden of response back to the interviewer. You should indicate that you are willing to stick by your original answer (whether it needs amplification or not), and that you are waiting for the interview to continue.

Remember: That eternity of silence is rarely as long as it seems—ten, fifteen, twenty seconds at the most. You should, however, prepare yourself for this possibility with a helpful partner, practice giving the silences back and gauging their length. The better you are prepared to meet these silences, the less intimidating they will seem during the actual interview.

Your interviewer may also do other things to put you off balance:

- Disagree with your opinions
- Challenge the truth of your statements
- Seem overly emotional
- Look displeased
- Act uninterested or dismissive

Don't let their mood influence yours! That is what handling stress is all about—answering any question without taking on the stress itself. The following exchange is a good example of this. A young applicant for a receptionist's job at a pharmaceutical firm was returning for what she thought would be a routine second interview with a member of the personnel department. It was anything but routine. Her interviewer kept emphasizing all the negative aspects of the job:

PERSONNEL: You know this is just a receptionist's job.

APPLICANT: That's all right—I like being a receptionist.

PERSONNEL: Think about it carefully. You will never go anywhere in this job—not at this company.

APPLICANT: That doesn't matter to me because I really do like being a receptionist. I'm good at it.

PERSONNEL: They told you that you wouldn't have a regular desk, didn't they? You'll be a floating receptionist, at a different desk every day.

APPLICANT: Yes, I consider that a plus. I'll get to meet everybody in the company and really know my job.

PERSONNEL: On Thursdays you will have to do mail room duty—the space is nothing more than a closet.

APPLICANT: It will be like my own little office—I can use the space well.

Unlike Mary, who was so rattled by Mr. Smith, this applicant didn't let the negative tone of the questions get her down. Whatever her interviewer gave to her, she gave it back, even upping the ante a little bit.

The more you can show the interviewer that you are able to hold your own and not let pressure get to you, the better you will come across in the interview. Although it is not always easy to do this, looking at such interviews as tests in and of themselves, and reminding yourself that they are not a reflection of you or your talents, are your best defenses in what can otherwise be a very difficult situation to handle successfully.

The Serial Interview

You may be required to have separate or "serial" interviews with a number of people, especially if you will be working for more than one boss, or if the position you are hired for is at a management level. The interviewers will see the applicants for a position separately and then get together to discuss their perceptions of the candidates and reach a consensus.

The important thing to remember is that you have to be consistent; don't tell one person one thing and change your story when you are talking to another. If your interviewers find any inconsistencies when they compare notes, it will not be looked on favorably. At best, you will be seen as unsure of yourself and, perhaps, unclear in your goals; at worst, they may suspect you of trying to hide something.

During these interviews, maintaining your level of enthusiasm will be hard, especially if you are seeing more than two people. Also, since no two individuals are alike, you will get on better with some than with others—and vice versa. That can't be helped. What you can do, however, is *not* write off someone who seems cool toward you and hope that you will do better with your next interviewer or be saved by your previous one. Concentrate on one interview at a time. Then, as soon as you've finished with that interview, put it of your mind and go on to your next interview.

Try to space out your questions over the entire series of interviews. This can be tricky. On the one hand, you don't want to ask the first person you see all the questions you have about the job and then have no questions left over for the interviewers down the line. On the other hand, you shouldn't ever stop yourself from asking questions; "saving" questions is never a good idea. In the first place, there is no guarantee that your next interviewer will answer them any more informatively. And if you've seen three people and ask the fourth some basic questions that you've been saving up, he may wonder why you are asking them at such a late date.

By and large, don't hold back—ask what's on your mind; chances are, as you begin interacting with the next interviewer, new questions will come to you. If they don't, summarize what you have learned and ask if this person agrees with it. For example: "As I understand it, I would be working for Miss Jones on Mondays and Tuesdays, for you on Wednesdays and Thursdays, and for Mr. Simms on Fridays. Is that correct?" You can also build upon your knowledge: "Is there anything else I should know about the schedule?" "Is this schedule flexible?" In effect, as an active interviewee, you should compare notes just as your interviewers will. The consistency required in a serial interview, has to work both ways. You want to make sure that what one person says matches what you have been told by someone else.

Board or Panel Interviews

"Board" or "panel" interviews tend to be very stressful because you are being interviewed by two, three, or more people at once. "I felt as though I were on trial," complained one grant applicant about a particularly difficult interview that took place at a university. "As soon as I answered one person's question, it always seemed as if somebody else was immediately ready to ask a follow-up question or disagree with what I had just said. I couldn't catch my breath."

That, in essence, is the difficulty with board interviews— because there are a number of people interviewing you, everything seems to happen very quickly. You can feel overwhelmed. Also, you become acutely aware that you can't please everybody. What may seem like the right answer to one person can alienate someone else.

Of course, that is what the board interview is all about. For the interviewers, it is a quick way of "getting at you." Your chances for recouping your energies after each question are slim, and your defenses come down more easily. And although it's a heightened experience, a board interview is an accurate representation of life— you will never be able to please everybody. In fact, the interviewers may want to see how you react in such a situation.

If you are just starting out in the job market, your chances of encountering such an interview are very slim. However, if you are applying for a grant or a position of responsibility with a nonprofit organization or in academia, you could very well be asked to come meet "the board," or any group of people in authority.

Your best defense during a board interview? Know your own mind. Accept the fact that not everyone will agree with you. Take their challenges as a matter of course. Be prepared to succinctly analyze and defend your points, but be wary of acting defensive or argumentative.

As with any regular interview, focus on those interviewing you, not on yourself. Direct your answer to whoever is asking you a particular question; don't get fixated on someone who appears to be the leader or the most supportive of you. Just like a serial interview, this is a stressful situation that also gives you the opportunity to interact with different people—except that here it happens all at once. You will have to try even harder to forget how you are coming across and focus on the questions at hand.

Although nervewracking, being called for a board interview is a good sign. It means that you have come far because the board is willing to invest its time in listening to what you have to say. So pat yourself on the back. Believe that what you have to offer the board is indeed useful, and use this knowledge to increase your self-confidence.

The Group Interview

In a group interview, you are one member of a group of people that is being interviewed. As in a board interview, the tension is heightened because there are so many people present. There is the additional factor of your relationship to other members of the group, who are also trying to get the job. Do you instinctively take a leadership role or defer to someone else? Do you defer to one particular person or all of them? What facets of your personality come out when you are placed in a group of people? How comfortable do you seem? These are all things that the people conducting the interview may think important to observe.

During the interview, the group may be given a problem to solve and the board members watch to see how different interviewees go about solving it. The way the interviewees react toward one another—as well as toward the interviewers—is also important. You may be asked theoretical questions and your answers may be challenged by the board members or by someone in your group. Or you may be challenged by a board member and supported by someone in your group or another board member. The possibilities multiply very quickly.

It is important to remember that in such a situation the board members are not necessarily looking for a take-charge type of leader. Perhaps they are looking for someone who can best build a consensus or someone who works well with one particular kind of person. Maybe it's a good listener they're after, rather than a big talker. What is important is that you not attempt to play any particular role but that you know your feelings about the various issues being considered so that you are not swayed by the behavior of others.

The Lunch Interview

If you have been asked on a lunch interview, you probably have already survived a screening interview and several other evaluations. Therefore, the best (and probably most difficult!) advice for you to follow is—relax.

Remember, you are being asked out to lunch for a reason. Your prospective boss (or bosses) is trying to get to know you better. This is both an extension of the office and a social occasion as well, so don't neglect one for the other. While you certainly want to keep the job in mind, you don't want it to interfere with your lunch either. Don't fall into the trap of obsessing about whether the people you are with will be watching your every action: how you use your knife, whether you know good wine from bad, how well you order from the menu. If you start worrying about infinitesimal details, you will defeat the purpose of the interview. Do whatever feels comfortable and keep your focus on getting to know your prospective boss and anyone else who might be present, just as they are focusing on getting to know you.

At the lunch, your companions may want to talk in greater depth about a particular problem discussed during the formal interview, or they may want to talk about something totally unrelated to work. Follow their lead, but don't be totally passive. If you feel that a particular topic should be brought up, do so. Remember, the tone of the lunch will depend on your participation as well as theirs. Above all, don't read too much into everything; remind yourself that maybe your hosts want to have a good time, too.

Here are a few general tips on staying relaxed during such a lunch:

- Order food that you are familiar with.
- Stay away from food that is difficult to eat or creates a mess easily.
- Don't be too self-conscious about alcohol, if you don't want any. Even if others are having drinks, feel free to decline; however, if no one is having alcohol, be wary of indulging.

- Don't be too self-conscious about ordering what your prospective boss is ordering—if you want it, order it; if not, don't.
- Don't criticize the food.
- Don't pick up the check. If you have checked your coat, however, that fee is your responsibility.

F I V E
. . . . .

The Interview:
First Impressions
Count

The most important part of the interview is its beginning. As soon as your prospective boss meets you, she forms an opinion of you based on the following: How you are dressed. How you carry yourself. What kind of authority you project. Whether you seem confident or nervous. You are telling people about yourself even before you say your first words. So you must think about how to project the best image of yourself from the first instant of the interview.

Your Arrival

Even your arrival can reveal something about yourself. You should plan to arrive about fifteen or twenty minutes early—traffic and public transportation problems can use up those minutes very quickly. If you haven't been to that particular office before, make sure you have good instructions on where it is located, including information on parking and the nearest public transportation. The last thing you want is to do is arrive late for an interview or make it just under the gun. If you do, you will feel flustered and have no time to compose yourself to do the work that needs to be done.

And it is work. It is during those initial minutes that you, as an active participant in your interview, will have to work hardest at focusing away from yourself and your fears and concentrating on the matter at hand: getting your thoughts together so you can best sell yourself to your prospective boss and find out about the job you are interviewing for.

This is not the time for more preparation. So try not to spend the time reviewing particular answers as though you were going over a math table in school; it is this rehearsed quality that makes answers sound canned. If you have gone over the various preparation procedures we have discussed and have decided on how you will present yourself, your answers will be there when you need them. Every interview is unique. Questions will be phrased differently and each will demand its own particular answer.

Instead, try to relax. Compose your thoughts. Taking

deep breaths will help steady your nerves and your voice. Once you have announced yourself to the receptionist, you may have to wait in the reception area for a few minutes before you are called in for the interview. To help relax, pick up a magazine or take out a book that you have brought with you. Does what you read count? Some people, feeling that they are being watched at all times, believe that they should only read serious material or something related to the company they are interviewing with. However, as with everything else, if you try too hard, it will show through. Don't read a trade journal if you have no interest in it. You will be posturing, not relaxing. Bring a book that you like or pick up a magazine that interests you instead of worrying whether it is serious enough. Aside from a few obvious extremes, most books and magazines will be appropriate.

What else should you bring with you to your interview?

- Your resume (one copy for each interview you expect to have, plus one extra just in case). You may already have distributed or sent in copies of your resume to the personnel department or your prospective boss. That doesn't matter; bring a few copies anyway. Resumes do get lost or filed away, and being well prepared never hurts.
- A small notebook and pen or pencil. While pens will always be provided, it is good to have your own. If you don't have one, some people will interpret it as a sign of helplessness. A notebook will come in handy should you want to write down any information: Again, having your own will show that you are prepared.

- A handkerchief or tissues. These will come in handy for any last minute grooming you may wish to do.

If you have time and it would make you feel more comfortable, ask the receptionist for the location of the restroom so you can check your appearance in the mirror. The extra bit of confidence you gain from knowing that you look fine just might tip the balance during those difficult moments of the interview when fear or insecurity may threaten your composure.

The Initial Meeting

Your initial meeting will be with the person who comes to the reception area to take you to the interview. If you are going for a screening interview, it will be a member of the personnel department. If you have already been screened and are headed for the formal job interview, this will be either someone from personnel, someone who works for the manager who will be interviewing you, or the interviewer herself. Generally, the larger the company, the more likely it is that you will be met by someone from personnel and taken through the interview process by that employee. Whoever it is, someone will always direct you to the next stop.

As mentioned previously, give due respect to everyone you meet; the personnel department may not have the power to hire you, but they have the power to reject you. Even if it is brief, your meeting with someone from personnel counts a lot.

To help allay your nervousness, try to notice the

physical environment as you are being led to your interviewer's office. You may be able to see how your potential co-workers' desks are arranged, what kind of office equipment they have, how much space has been allotted for them. Even if you only get a fleeting glimpse, these impressions may lead to your asking some pertinent questions during the interview.

Your first introduction to your interviewer is all-important. If there is any time that you want to look "up"—enthusiastic, warm, friendly—it is now. You shake hands. Some things never go out of style—a quick, firm handshake is still desirable. Look your interviewer in the eye. Smile. Friendliness and accessibility are what you want to convey now.

If your interviewer is like most people, she will try to put you at ease and motion you to a chair. If you have the presence of mind to do so, try to notice things about your interviewer and the office as you settle in: Are there pictures on the walls or gadgets on the desk that show a particular interest or hobby? Is everything arranged just so or do the surroundings betray a certain informality? Does anything in particular strike you immediately upon entering: artwork, a piece of furniture, even the view out the window? Whatever you can pick out will help you to take your mind off yourself and it will also provide clues about the kind of person you are meeting with. As the interview progresses, you might be able to work something about what you notice into your conversation.

A good bit of advice comes from one personnel recruiter who said: "When applicants walk in the door, I'm not happy when they act as though they are in a glass bubble. I want to feel that they are noticing what is around them: examples of the products we sell on the shelves, awards, the huge ficus plants I have in the corners of my office. I certainly don't expect them to comment about everything, but I do like getting that sense that people are aware of things."

Off and Running—
The Interview Begins

Always respond to questions as though your interview has already begun—because it has!

Some interviewers will begin by making small talk with you as you are getting settled, to allow you to get better acquainted. Others will jump right in and ask a question. For some, the small talk itself is part of the interview, to see how you respond to seemingly innocuous questions. You have to be prepared for all enventualities.

You also have to be prepared for anything from a rigidly structured interview to one that seems much looser, or without any structure at all. In a structured interview, your interviewer will have a list of questions, either written or memorized. You will be asked the questions and expected to answer accordingly; usually these are on topics directly related to your job search. In a less structured interview, your interviewer will take more cues from you—talking about topics you bring up, digressing a bit, and generally acting more like an acquaintance than an interviewer. While such an interview gives you more of an opportunity to express yourself, it is also trickier. Lulled by its informal atmosphere, you may unintentionally ramble or reveal things you did not mean to.

By and large, as the interview progresses, you can expect your interviewer to do about one third of the talking and you about two thirds. This will vary, of course, especially in the beginning, as you and your interviewer both struggle to get a feel for each other. Use the one-third to two-thirds ratio only as a general guide—much will depend on how directed the interview is. The important thing is that you do not fool yourself into thinking that the interview will start at a particular time—like when your interviewer asks one of those standard questions about your career path or your previous experience. Always respond to questions as though your interview has already begun—because it has!

If right off the bat your interviewer tosses out what appears to be a difficult or complex question you may be in for a stress interview. Assume as much, take a breath, and jump right in yourself. This is part of the interviewer's game—to see how well you keep up.

By the way, there is nothing wrong with trying to gain some time if you need it. If you do get hit with an unexpected or difficult question—either now or at any time during the interview—you can always say, "That's a difficult question" or "Well, let me think about that for a second." There is nothing wrong with taking a few seconds to compose your thoughts. Remember: silence always feels much longer when you have someone staring at you, waiting for you to say something. Just as giving back a silence shows your mettle, asking for some time to think will show your interviewer that you respect yourself enough to ask for the time to answer a question adequately.

Your demeanor throughout the entire interview carries a lot of weight. The way to convey as professional a demeanor as possible is not to *do* anything in particular but to *think* well of yourself. Focus on your strengths and on your positive attributes, and your demeanor will automatically convey your positive thoughts. You have prepared well, so you will do well in this interview; you have good qualifications and a solid background; you like the company and feel that this job is for you. However, be careful of exhibiting the following habits and behavioral tics that convey nervousness or other negative qualities:

- Slouching
- Staring off into space
- Fidgeting
- Playing with hair, fingers, clothes, jewelry
- Tapping feet
- Checking the time

And of course, during the interview, don't smoke or chew gum. Neither of these will be appreciated.

Recovering from a Bad Beginning

Occasionally, despite your best efforts, the beginning of the interview will not go very well. You may sense an immediate coolness between yourself and the person who is interviewing you. Something may happen in the office—such as an emergency—to distract either of you. You may not be feeling well and therefore have difficulty concentrating. Or you may initially give what you think is a bad answer or an inappropriate response to a question and feel doomed from that point on.

The unfortunate thing in such situations is that you can let the initial problem color your entire interview. Then, instead of putting your best foot forward, you sink lower and lower into yourself and write off the interview before you've given it a real chance to succeed. Your responses to questions become perfunctory or labored, and you begin to give off the unmistakable impression that you want to leave as quickly as possible. Your interviewer will sense this, and more often than not will grant you your wish and write you off as well.

Your first step in combatting this unfortunate set of circumstances is to identify that it is happening. If you start feeling sorry for yourself or in any way thinking negatively—"Oh, I blew this," "She doesn't like me, I can just tell she doesn't like me"—*stop*, before you drive more nails into the coffin.

Once you recognize that you are doing this, acknowledge it—verbally if you can. While difficult, stopping the interview and acknowledging the problem to your interviewer can win you points. With this acknowledgment, however, you should give an explanation of why you feel you weren't on the ball and what you consider to be a better answer. If you were to say, "I'm sorry, I really feel I didn't adequately explain why I want the job because I was still focused on your first question about the art of selling," you just may get the interview back on the right track. Your explanation of the problem should be specific, and your answer should be different from what you said before, and delivered with conviction. This usually works best when, for whatever reason, you have given a so-so answer to a question and then suddenly think of a much better response.

Be careful, however, with this type of verbal backtracking: Use it no more than once and only for a question of major import. If you begin constantly correcting yourself or offering explanations for your inability to concentrate, the interviewer may feel sorry for you but will not be inclined to offer you the job. No matter how convincing your excuses—and that's what they are, excuses—the person behind the desk can't help but wonder if your excuses will continue after you have been hired.

More often than not, your acknowledgment that you are sinking into a negative pattern will be nonverbal. If you sense a definite coolness in your interviewer's manner, for example, it would not be wise to bring this out into the open directly: Doing so could easily be interpreted as confrontational—not the attitude you want to convey. Act as you would if you were in a stress interview: Give yourself a moment, put your interviewer's cool manner or your bad answer behind you, and focus on the future. Tell yourself that you still have most of the interview in which to "show your stuff." Pretend you just walked in and are starting from scratch. Get angry at yourself for forgetting all your good points. Whatever you do, let go of that defeatist attitude—what do you have to lose? If your interviewer is cool toward you, that's her problem, not yours. If she sounds curt and demeaning, maybe she's having a bad day. If you can lift your spirits, even a notch, your answers will come more quickly and be sharper and more focused. The improvement in your attitude alone will win you points.

Occasionally, you will realize only after you've left the interview that you have not done well. If you really think the job is for you, call up the personnel department of the company at which you interviewed. Again, be ready with a good explanation of why you feel you deserve a second chance and have a list of specific points that you want to bring up now, but that you failed to bring up previously. Your determination will be looked upon favorably; and if you can back it up with convincing reasons, you just may succeed in giving yourself a second, real chance.

Building Rapport—Consider the Interviewer's Point of View

In order to make the best use of those precious first few minutes, think a bit about how things look from the interviewer's point of view. He has probably seen a few people already and may be tired or even bored with describing the same job, going over the same duties, asking prospective employees the same questions, and listing to similar responses. The interviewer also has his own job and may feel pressured to get back to the "real" work that needs to be done. And although the questions he asks and the answers you give are important, he will also hire someone based on his gut feelings: If you *feel* right, you will get the job offer. Is there anything you can do to influence this decision?

While much of the success of the interviewer will depend on the chemistry between the two of you— something over which you have little control—you can influence the process by establishing a rapport as much as possible. See if you can get the interviewer to open up by opening up yourself. For example, use what you noticed upon coming into the office and relate it to one of your hobbies or personal experiences. Ask questions. Make observations. Don't be afraid of remarking on something. It may feel like you are taking a bit of a chance because you are not strictly answering the questions that are put to you, but that is what being a power interviewee is all about: not only answering the questions but expanding on them. The trick is in finding the connections to the topics you are discussing. If you can work your observations and experiences into the discussion, you are taking much less of a chance than you think. And you just may hit upon something that gets your interviewer to open up and helps establish a real rapport between you.

In trying to establish rapport, be careful of becoming

too comfortable or giving cute answers; these can back-fire as well. Remember that this is a professional situation and you have to act accordingly. If you are able to build rapport, however, both of you will be energized by it. It's the best way to stand out from the pack.

S I X
_____

. . . . .

The Give and Take: Keep the Ball in Your Court

As an active interviewee, always remember that it is a two-way street: You have as much right to ask questions as the interviewer has.

You've met your interviewer, have suffered through the awkwardness of being introduced, and perhaps you've exchanged some initial pleasantries. And now you are really getting down to business. You're in the heart of the interview, discussing the ins and outs of the job, your qualifications, and your interests. As a successful interviewee, always remember that it is a two-way street: You have as much right to ask questions as your interviewer has. While the interviewer wants to know more about you, you want to know more about the job. The questions your interviewer asks and the questions that you pose are the give and take of the interview. And during this process of give and take, you can do things to influence the course of the interview to your benefit.

The most important thing in this process is to be aware of what is *really* behind the questions your interviewer poses to you. The better you understand this hidden agenda, the better you can give answers that will lead the interview in the direction you want it to go. The same thing holds true for what you ask your interviewer: the more you have thought about what to ask and how to ask it, the more you will find out about the job and whether it is really for you.

The Questions They Ask— The Hidden Agenda

The type of questioning we normally associate with interviews—"what-are-your-strengths-and-weaknesses" and "tell-me-about-your-career-plans"—is on the wane. This has been replaced by what is most commonly referred to as "behavioral" interviewing or "targeted selection" or "problem-solving" interviewing. Whatever it's called, its main purpose is to get you to talk about yourself in depth. Your interviewer is still interested in your strengths and weaknesses; however he knows that if he asks a question like that directly, you will tend to give a rehearsed response, something he does not want to hear. Instead, he will try to find out about your strengths and weaknesses indirectly, by giving you a problem to solve, asking you to describe your accomplishments, or asking how you dealt with difficult situations in previous jobs.

This is why the self-inventory and the preparation discussed earlier are so crucial. While specific questions cannot, and should not, be anticipated, the different aspects of your professional life that are an interviewer's main concerns should be thought through carefully. And the better you can anticipate those concerns, the better prepared you will be to answer questions, no matter how they are put to you.

In behavioral interviewing, your interviewer will often give you a specific problem in your area of expertise and ask how you would go about solving it. The problem could focus on your abilities at working with other people or test your knowledge in a particular area. For example, a typical question might be, "How would you go about raising sales of product X, which is losing ground to product Y?" The way you propose to solve this problem shows your interviewer how you work—the way you think, how you arrive at your decisions, what you do with the knowledge you have. Thus, instead of providing a list of your strengths and weaknesses, you have revealed them indirectly.

As you are answering questions, be aware of the following concerns that may be on your interviewer's mind:

Confidence and decision-making skills. It is a cliché that we live and work in a world filled with pressure. Many jobs require the ability to make quick decisions in difficult situations, and many interviewers are particularly concerned that you display the confidence not only to make those decisions but to stick with them. If the job you are interviewing for involves working with many people or is conducted in a high-pressure atmosphere, be prepared to be put on the spot by such questions as:

- "Before leaving for two weeks, I ask you to do a report for me due on the first day I return. The information for that report comes from persons A, B and C. When you begin, however, you find out that person A is away for one week and person C, for two weeks. What do you do?"
- "Tell me about a difficult situation in your previous job and how you handled it."
- "Why should I hire you rather than anyone else I've seen?"

There are no right or wrong answers to these questions. What is right is that you show the interviewer that you know your own mind and don't appear to be helpless. If a job is to be particularly demanding, don't be surprised if a stress interview ensues. Remember, play along with the game and don't take the stress on—that is exactly what your interviewer is looking for.

Priorities Related to your ability to make difficult decisions is your ability to prioritize them. What you choose to do and why will tell your interviewer what you consider important; it will also reveal certain facets of your personality. Know which aspects of your personality you want the interviewer to see and watch for questions such as the following:

- "If you work for Mr. Jones and Miss Smith and they both ask you to do something right away, how do you respond?"
- "What would you do first on a given day: fire your incompetent assistant or call your boss to tell her you've just come up with a way to save the company millions of dollars?"
- "What do you like about your current job and why?"

Organizational skills. Instead of asking whether you are organized, which would prompt an obvious yes, an interviewer may ask wide-open questions that can be answered in a number of different ways. If the interviewer is curious about your organizational abilities, he will be looking for how many things you juggle at once, whether you complain of being overwhelmed, how you organize the very answer you are giving at the moment. Watch for inquiries into your organizational abilities contained in questions such as:

- "Describe the company where you work now."
- "What is a busy day at your current job? How do you deal with it?"
- "What are your primary and/or secondary duties?"

Teamwork. Questions revolving around teamwork are designed to see how well you would fit in with your potential co-workers. Since the concepts of teamwork and team building are gaining more and more importance, don't be surprised to be asked such questions as:

- "How would you go about choosing the best employees to work on Project X?"
- "What kinds of people do you like to work with?"

67

- "How have you helped your co-workers accomplish their goals?"
- "What do you consider the most important qualities for a successful employee in our industry?"

As you can see, in answering these questions, you are not only indicating the kinds of people you feel comfortable with, but by implication you are revealing a lot of yourself. So use such occasions to sell yourself to your best advantage. Always keep in mind that the interviewer is concentrating on you while you are concentrating on responding to the question.

Initiative. When your interviewer asks, "Why do you want to work for our company?" he may also be curious to know what you know about the company. Giving a well thought-out answer will show that you have done your research, which in turn will show your initiative. The extent to which you went out of your way to find out about the company is a true indication of how much you really do want that job.

Everyone likes motivated employees and interviewers look for signs of initiative by asking all sorts of questions: Keep in mind those occasions that bring out this quality in you—what you did in previous jobs that was above and beyond the call of duty, any volunteer or committee work you have been involved in, instances where you've shown that you can take charge and get things done. They can come up in answering questions such as the following:

- "How would you describe your method of working?"

- "Tell me about a project that failed. Why did it fail? How did you react?"
- "How does your current job/position differ now from when you first started?"

Ambition. Asking about your goals and accomplishments is a good way to measure your ambition and to test how well you would fit into the structure of the company. These questions can focus on past achievements or things you want to accomplish in the future.

- "What is your proudest achievement?"
- "Where do you see yourself two years, five years from now?"
- "What do you see as the most important function of this job?"

Questions such as these allow you an opportunity to position yourself in a way that will fit in with the company's needs. If you tell your interviewer, "I see myself running a similar company five years from now," in answer to the second question, you are saying that you are ambitious and do not plan to stay around forever. Depending on the position you are interviewing for at present, that may or may not be the best answer. Be aware that while initiative is always desirable, ambition can cut two ways; no one wants employees so ambitious that they ignore the company's needs for their own.

Confidentiality. It is not a good idea to tattle on your old boss or previous company. If you feel that you were mistreated, that your previous boss was difficult to work for, or that your old company had serious problems, an interview is not the place to complain about it. In the first place, your interviewer will never be sure whether or not this is the whole story, as it is only coming from you, and may wonder whether your boss or co-workers would give a totally different reading of the situation. Secondly, he may worry that you will do the same thing to him in some future interview.

So, be wary of such questions as:

- "What do you and your boss disagree on most strongly?"
- "Why aren't you looking for a promotion at your present firm?"
- "What do you dislike about your present job?"

If you feel that certain problems are an important part of your decision to leave, state them, but do so as objectively as possible—this is not the time for revenge. Going off on a tirade about the horrible abuses heaped upon you in your previous job will backfire. Your interviewer will remember your anger rather than any specific problems you talk about and may come to the conclusion that you are difficult to get along with. Work through all your feelings of being wronged during your preparation period and try to see the other point of view. Then in the interview you can refer to those problems in a calm, detached manner.

Be wary also if you sense the interview turning into an information-gathering session by a competitor. If you find yourself talking about sensitive topics—the current sales figures of your old firm, the way certain departments operate, financial problems, or any gossip you have heard—*stop*. Whether such information is solicited deliberately or because the interviewer is inexperienced, it has no place in any job interview.

And never be seduced into thinking that by offering certain juicy tidbits of information, you will get a better shot at the job. An honest interviewer will be put off immediately, and someone who is after such information won't owe you anything once you have spilled the beans. Also, remember that many industries are smaller than you think: your interviewer may be good friends with someone in your present company. Trying to win over a new firm by airing the dirty laundry of your old one can easily come back to haunt you. Not only will you not get the new job, you may lose your old one.

Being Fired and Other Liabilities

We all have our weaknesses, and fear of their exposure is usually what makes interviews so daunting. We imagine that just when we least expect it, the interviewer will ask The Question: Why is there a time gap in your resume? Why were you fired from job X? Why did you stay in this job so long? Can we call company Y to verify your salary? These recommendations?

During an interview our instinct, of course, is to gloss over anything we feel will not stand us in good stead. We usually rationalize this tendency to cover up any unpleasantness by convincing ourselves that it is easier not to deal with the truth at all than to try to make the interviewer believe our side of the story. In some cases this is true; in others, it isn't. In most cases, the truth cannot be avoided and we have to deal with it in one way or another. There are, however, good ways to confront some of the common liabilities we take into interviews.

Being fired. It is always a big problem to have been fired, and you will have to confront this fact during the interview unless you spent a short time at the company that you can leave the job off your resume, or it happened so long ago that it doesn't really matter anymore. If you do omit the job from your resume, you have to make sure that someone reading it will detect no obvious gaps in time. As explained earlier, in this instance it may help if you have a functional, rather than chronological, resume. It will also be easier to omit the job if it was in a different field or a totally different geographical location from where you are interviewing at present. But if it is in the same field, hiding the fact that you were fired will be more difficult because of the information network that exists in many industries. With a little bit of checking, the management at the company you are interviewing with will find out the truth.

Usually, the fact of having been fired will loom large during any interview you may have. Here are some tips on confronting it:

- Let your interviewer bring it up. Don't volunteer the information too readily; there is a chance that it won't come up during your interview.
- Don't skirt around it when it does come up. If you see the conversation going in that direction, don't avoid the issue. Hesitation and hedging your bets

never get you points in an interview; confronting something head on is always more impressive.

- Be prepared with a good defense. Think through all sides of the story and try to find some logical explanation for why that particular job did not work out. Instead of pointing fingers and assigning blame, find reasons why the fit was not good.

- List your reasons dispassionately. As we discussed, it is important to avoid sounding vengeful. A calm, rational discussion of the matter will sound much more believable than an angry tirade.

- Have another person at your old company vouch for you. If someone who worked with you will give you a good recommendation, it will go far in countering the effects of being fired. Of course, the more closely you worked with that person, and the more responsibility he or she had, the better.

- If there is any truth in it, try to give reasons that are tied more to the company's performance rather than yours: the company was cutting back staff, there were budgetary problems, the job had a high turn-over rate, the nature of the job changed.

- Turn the experience into something positive. Try to think of what it taught you—how you've changed because of it, what you've learned, and how you can apply this knowledge in the future.

- If you've held a number of positions since then and have received good reviews in all of them, the firing will not be a big problem—and it may not even come up during your interview. Nevertheless, you still want to review the facts and prepare a good defense ahead of time should you be questioned about it.

Fudging experience and degrees. If you want a job badly enough, it is tempting to fudge certain facts in order to present yourself as fully qualified. However, glossing over deficiencies in experience or education is never a good idea. Even if you get the job, lying can have repercussions far down the road. In the first place, colleges and universities do give out information on degrees they have awarded; all a company has to do is call the registrar's office to find out if indeed you got the degree you said you did. Many firms make it a policy to automatically fire someone who has knowingly lied about such matters—even if it's years down the road. Your degree may not matter at first, but you may need proof of it if you are up for a promotion, if routine checks are done on employees, or if the company changes hands. The same holds true for skills and experience. If it is discovered that you don't know something you claimed you did, you may suffer anything from minor embarrassment to being fired for misrepresentation.

If you try to gloss over any lack of education or experience, a good interviewer will see through this very quickly. Instead of making up experience you don't have, admit your lack and try to think of what you have to offer that can offset it: experience that is similar (give specific examples); the strengths particular to your background that would be useful in the job; what you can do to augment your qualifications, such as taking courses or seminars. If the rest of the interview is going well, showing such determination just might tip the balance in your favor.

Listing your weaknesses. Even in a behavioral interview, you should be prepared for a direct question about your weaknesses because it still does get asked. Your interviewer may do this if he is pressed for time, decides to add some more stress to the process, or is just plain curious. And since the question is so direct and unexpected, it sometimes elicits a painfully true response in the unprepared interviewee.

What are your options in responding to this old standby? You can't say you have no weaknesses because you won't be believed. But if you sincerely start listing all the areas in your professional life in which you are sorely lacking, you just may talk yourself out of a job. Instead try, if you can do so honestly, to turn your weaknesses into strengths; that is, carefully think about where you are lacking and try to find something about it that can actually be perceived as a strength. Some typical responses:

- I'm very hard on myself.
- I'm a perfectionist.
- I don't let go of work easily.
- I drive myself/my assistant too much.

Have specific examples and anecdotes to back up such claims—the more you have the more you will be believed.

Conflict with your boss. Rightly or wrongly, your relationship with your old boss carries a lot of weight with every interviewer. If you had a conflict with your current or previous boss and if for any reason it comes up in an interview—you are asked about references, you refer to the conflict when answering a question, the interviewer already has that information—be prepared with an explanation.

The generic excuse of "personality conflict" cannot be used as a blanket statement. It requires elaboration. The interviewer will want to know the nature of the conflict, how it developed, and why it festered. In many respects, dealing with this problem is similar to dealing with having been fired. Don't bring it up yourself, but don't avoid the issue if your interviewer brings it up. Explain the conflict from all sides and do not use the opportunity as a forum for revenge. If you can get someone else who supervised you to put in a good word for you, it will always help a great deal.

Dealing with Illegal Questions

Unless directly related to the job you are interviewing for, the following areas of your life are off limits to an interviewer:

- Marital status or marital plans
- Plans for children
- Age
- Religion
- Political affiliations
- Your personal finances or credit rating
- A criminal record
- Questions about your nationality or culture
- Questions of a sexual nature

Anti-discrimination laws vary from state to state, but

the general thrust of all such laws is to prevent a potential employer from discriminating against you for reasons that have nothing to do with your suitability for a particular job. If you feel you have been discriminated against, you can contact the Equal Employment Opportunity Commission (EEOC), a federal agency set up to handle such matters. Its 800 number is listed in the blue pages of the phone book under United States government agencies. When you call you will get a recording that provides information on how to go about filing a complaint or getting recourse for discrimination. The time limit for filing a complaint is 180 days.

You have two choices in dealing with such questions about your personal life during the interview. If you feel the interviewer is touching upon such issues in an inappropriate way, you can refuse to answer. You have every right to do this, and depending on how intrusive you find such questioning, you may feel you have no other recourse. Of course, speaking your mind may very well destroy any rapport the two of you have built up and minimize your chances for getting the job.

Usually, leaving your options open—keeping that ball in your court—is the better strategy. First, try to get that job. If you answer what you believe is an illegal question and you get a job offer, you still have the choice of lodging a complaint or dismissing the incident. The decision will be yours and you will not have prematurely shut the door on your chances.

The Questions You Ask—What You Are Entitled to Know

Never be afraid of the questions you may have

You should always have questions for your interviewer. They are a sign that you are sincerely interested in the job because you are motivated to find out what you can about it. Your interviewer may not always remember your specific questions, but she will always remember that you had some.

Of course, the best questions, like the best responses, are not canned but come naturally from the conversation you are having with your interviewer. If you have established a rapport and the give and take is real, you will naturally want further clarification of certain aspects of the job, specific examples of certain things you have discussed, a better picture of where you will fit into the department or the company as a whole. If these questions come to mind while talking to your interviewer, ask them. Never be afraid of the questions you may have. Remember, no one expects you to have all the answers or know all the ins and outs of any new job. If you did, it wouldn't be the job for you—you would already have outgrown it.

While you are preparing for the interview, it is a good idea to write down your questions in the little notebook that you will be carrying with you. Although, hopefully, new questions will come up during the interview, your little notebook is a perfectly legitimate interviewing aid. If you can't remember all the questions on your list, feel free to ask the interviewer if it would be okay to take out the notebook and quickly review your questions. Your interviewer won't mind; it's another small detail that shows you've taken the interview seriously. Even if you don't need to refer to the notebook, knowing you have it with you will give you that much more confidence.

During your interview, you are entitled to find out about following: the duties and responsibilities of the job; the overall goals of the company or department you will be working for; what happened to your predecessor; opportunities for growth; the working environment; and problem areas.

The duties and responsibilities of the job. The most important topic covered during the interview. In discussing the job, make sure you are clear on

- Who you will be reporting to
- Who will be reporting to you
- The lines of authority
- Your duties
- What your priorities will be (knowing what your prospective boss considers your most important tasks gives you a good indication of the nature of your job)
- What meetings you are expected to attend and your responsibilities at those meetings

You are also entitled to know how much overtime is expected of you. If you are interviewing for a management position, overtime can include social activities such as entertaining clients at dinners, out-of-town trips and conventions, or various social gatherings and publicity events. If the job involves long hours, your interviewer should tell you up front. If she doesn't, inquire about it. Feel free to ask specific questions: About how many hours per week of overtime? Are any months of the year particularly busy? Are there any particular duties that will require extra effort?

If you are asked whether overtime will be a problem, know what you will say. Try to think through beforehand how much overtime you will accept or under what conditions it will not be a problem for you. In discussing overtime it is hemming and hawing that gives a negative impression. If you hesitate when told that a certain amount of overtime is expected, that will be seen as foot dragging, an indication that you won't want to pitch in and help.

The overall goals of the company or department you will be working for. Asking questions about the larger picture shows that you want more than just any job. It indicates that you care about fitting in with your co-workers and shows that you have your own goals and expectations in life. It is also a good way to show your initiative and that you have done your homework.

Just be careful that you don't overreach. Some general questions about the company (its main products and services, how it has been doing recently) are fine. It is when you start showing off your knowledge and begin asking questions about aspects of the company that wouldn't have anything to do with your job that you get into trouble.

Some questions to ask:

- "Has our department/company grown in the last few years? How?"

- "Where do we fit in? In the company? In the industry?"
- "Do you have an overall philosophy for the department/company?"
- "What kind of person succeeds in this department/company?"

What happened to your predecessor. Although your predecessor's career will not necessarily reflect yours, you can still find out a lot from the answers the interviewer gives you. If the comments about your predecessor seem positive, ask what your interviewer liked about working with this person. If the comments seem negative, you have to tread more carefully. Instead of inquiring about your predecessor's faults, put the focus on yourself: Ask if there is anything in particular that your interviewer would want you to do in order to create a more positive working relationship.

What are the opportunities for growth. In discussing promotion possibilities, you are always walking a fine line between seeming overly eager and not motivated enough. Remember that your interviewer has a particular job to fill; it is that job you should show the most interest in. As far as your interviewer is concerned, if you do well in that job, the future will take care of itself. So while you should seem eager and motivated, you also don't want to give the impression that you will get bored quickly and leave. Your research can greatly help you to walk that fine line. If you have a general idea of how long a person in such a position is expected to stay, you will have an appropriate response if your interviewer questions your interest in future promotions:

say that you just want to make sure your expectations match the reality of the situation.

Working environment. You want to get some sense of what your working day will be like. This can be influenced by your physical space, the way your boss or department functions, the machinery and support systems you will use in your job.

As mentioned earlier, you should try to get a sense of the company environment while you are being ushered into your interview. Don't be afraid to ask about what you noticed on the way in. If you feel self-conscious about asking questions about something that seems to be a relatively minor factor in choosing a job, do so in a way that implies you are just clarifying what you saw: "Will I be working right at that desk outside your office?" "Will my office be in the area I passed through on my way in?" "Will it be possible to take a look at it on my way out?"

You will also want to know the preferred mode of working. Ask how your interviewer likes to work and how she likes the employees to work. How independent should someone in your position be? How should you offer feedback? On a case-by-case basis? By written reports? In weekly meetings? What kinds of deadlines are there in your job? What other employees will you be interacting with? For what purposes?

In certain jobs, machinery and support systems are very important. If you're used to working with a particular computer or other piece of equipment, make sure you inquire about its availability. Determine beforehand how you will answer if it is not available. And ask about help. If you are particularly busy, are there other workers who can ease some of the burden? Whom can you turn to? Also, asking about help is a good way to find out about overtime and determine how much of the midnight oil you really will have to burn.

Problem areas. Just as your interviewer can ask you about your liabilities, as a successful interviewee you have every right to find out about any problems the job may have. In asking about problems, remember that turnabout is fair play. If your interviewer hesitates in answering or seems to be covering up something, beware. Maybe you're not getting the full story.

There are a few things to consider:

- The job has a high turnover rate. If your interviewer mentions this, try to find out why. Ask if your predecessors left of their own accord. If the answer is no, a polite way to find out more information is to inquire whether your interviewer couldn't find the right person for the job. What you want to rule out, of course, is some inherent problem: There is a discrepancy between the authority given to the person in the position and the duties they are expected to carry out, your boss is temperamental or unduly demanding, others in the organization are difficult to work with. Since you cannot ask these things directly, focus your questions on the people in the job: What qualities were they lacking? What should they have done that they didn't do? Did they ignore a particular person or department?
- Your interviewer seems unenthusiastic or doesn't know much about the job. Explore further. If the

interviewer doesn't have a good grasp of the job—is hesitant, isn't sure of the duties involved, gives incomplete answers—this vagueness may hide deeper problems either in the department or the company. Your interviewer's own position in the company may be precarious. He may not have a good working relationship with the staff. The company itself may be in turmoil. Tread carefully in such a situation. Chances are you don't want the job.

- If you have a particular problem in your current job, make sure to bring it up during the interview. If, for example, you are having trouble getting information from others, which makes it difficult for you to do your job, ask how a similar situation is handled in this company. While we have acknowledged that an interview is not an occasion for revenge, referring to a particular problem without naming names or getting into too many specifics is perfectly legitimate. As long as you focus on the problem and its affect on your job, you are well within the bounds of propriety.

SEVEN

The Finish: Negotiating Salary and the Follow Up

At some point during the give and take of the interview, you will know whether you are interested in the job or not. You will have to communicate this to your interviewer. If you are not interested, you should say so and politely state your reasons. This will save both of you time and further needless questioning. After thanking your interviewer for seeing you, prepare to be escorted out.

If you feel that this particular job is not for you but that you would be interested in pursuing other jobs in the company, don't be afraid to say so and treat the interview as a form of networking. Give your interviewer a quick summary of why you like the company and what jobs

you think you can do. A good word from your interviewer to the personnel department will weigh very
heavily when an appropriate position does come up in the
future.

If you are interested in the position you are interviewing for, first summarize your understanding of what the
position entails—"From our conversation, I understand
the job to involve the following: . . ."; "From what
you've told me, the job entails. . . ." Then say why
you want it and would be good at it—"I really would
enjoy the position because . . ."; "I think I would bring
to the position the following strengths: . . ."

A word of caution: Keep your options open. Express-
ing your *interest* in a job, no matter how strong, is not an
official acceptance of it or commitment to take it. Before
you can accept a job, you must be offered it. After
you've expressed interest, it is up to the company to
officially extend the offer. Be careful if your interviewer
says something on the order of, "Will you take the job if
we offer it to you?" She may be just trying to keep her
options open, too. So don't box yourself in; put the
responsibility back on her shoulders by reiterating your
interest and asking if she is indeed offering you the job or
when she plans to do so.

Another reason for keeping your options open, of
course, is salary, which is traditionally discussed at the
end of the interview. If the interview has gone well and
both you and the interviewer have shown strong interest
in working together, you will try to come to an agreement
on an acceptable salary. It is usually the last big stum-
bling block to landing a job.

Negotiating Salary

Ideally, you want to go into any job interview having a good idea of the salary range for that job. Of course, having exact figures is not always possible because salary depends on so many factors: what the official range is at that particular company, how flexible the company is in bending the rules, how impressive your qualifications seem to your prospective boss, and how much influence she has in bending any rules. Generally, the higher the position, the more flexible the salary. If you are just starting out, expect that the salary range for the job will be fairly consistent for all companies within that particular industry. Don't expect your prospective boss to put her professional life on the line for you; if you don't like the salary, think about another industry or position altogether.

There are different ways to research salary ranges.

- Ask about salaries during informational interviews.
- Study want ads for similar positions (some list salary ranges).
- Ask friends or acquaintances who are in the business.
- Use the library (research books on various industries; find articles in newspapers or magazines on salary trends).
- Attend seminars or adult education courses on various industries (even if salaries are not on the official agenda, your teacher or someone you meet may give you valuable information).
- Check out college placement offices and school guidance counselors.

While the methods above may not provide you with exact figures, you will nevertheless get some idea of what to expect. Certainly, the more research you do, the more realistic your expectations will be and the more confidence you will have in your decision whether to accept a given salary or hold out for more money.

The most important thing to remember in negotiating salary is that you should not commit yourself to a particular salary first; before saying anything, try to get your interviewer to give you a figure or a range. If you state your expectations right away, you may make yourself vulnerable by giving a figure that is too low or too high. If it is too low, you will be selling yourself short. If you name a figure that is too high, it will be hard to backtrack and you may lose your chances for the job.

If the interviewer puts you on the spot and asks you to state your salary expectations, you can try to put the question back to her. Feign ignorance: "That is something I've been meaning to ask you because I am not sure. What does the job pay?" Or emphasize your strengths: "From what we've discussed, I think I could do a great job for you. Taking my qualifications into account, what salary can I expect?"

Discussions about money make most interviewees so uncomfortable that they tend to accept whatever salary is being offered rather than actually do any negotiating. Look at salary discussions as yet another element of stress to parry back and forth with your interviewer. If you are able to treat questions about money in such a way, you may not only get a better salary but you will also earn respect for your good negotiating skills.

If for whatever reasons you are forced to state your

salary expectations first, try to give a figure that you believe is high. If the figure is way out of the ballpark, you may have to suffer the embarrassment of being told that you are naïve, but at least you will not be selling yourself short. And remember that *expectation* is the key word here. Unless you are very sure of yourself, don't put the figure in terms of the minimum you can *accept*. If your interviewer can't match that figure and you've said you can't accept anything lower, you will not be able to negotiate down. However, if you have stated that your figure is an expectation, you have left room for further negotiation. Keeping the door open is the key to all successful negotiating.

When you are given a salary figure, whether first or in response to yours, remember that your interviewer is offering the lowest figure she thinks she can get away with. In the ensuing discussions, that figure will only go up, not down.

Also, be aware of how much your previous salary will influence your discussions. If you are changing jobs for more money, a salary jump of about 15 to 20 percent is a reasonable expectation. Your interviewer will know what your previous salary was, so if you are seeking an increase of much more than 20 percent, you should have good reasons to back up your demands. (This holds true if by chance your previous salary was higher than what is now being offered. Reasons for going into lower-paying jobs can be very legitimate—such as a desire to change industries or the need to reduce the stress in your life— but be prepared to explain yourself thoroughly on that score.)

Once your interviewer names a figure, you have to be

very clear on how much you will compromise. Making quick decisions during the heat of an interview is difficult. To gain some time, tell the interviewer that based on your qualifications—or your research—you were hoping for X amount, and increase the amount being offered by whatever percentage you feel comfortable. Your interviewer may say that she'll see what can be done. Or she may tell you it's impossible and wait for your response. It's back to you—the cycle begins again. You will then have to decide whether to accept the offer or hold out for money.

In deciding how to respond to a salary offer, you have to consider the following:

- How badly you want the job. You just may not be able to get more money. Are you ready to accept this possibility?
- How sure you are of what such a position pays. The better your research, the stronger your negotiating stance.
- How well the interview has gone. If the interviewer has seemed very excited about you and has indicated that you are a strong choice, you have more reason to hold out for more money.

But keep in mind that nothing is guaranteed. You may be a strong choice but the next interviewee may be stronger. Negotiation always involves an element of risk; it is your bluff against the other person's.

In discussing salary, your other difficulty is that in most cases you will not get a commitment during the interview. Even if your interviewer indicates that she may be able to get more money for you, chances are she won't do it right there and then. If you feel strongly that you can't take the job unless you get a better offer, you will have to follow through on your decision and leave the interview without a firm commitment. If you are very interested in the job, this can be very difficult to do.

Once questions of salary have been resolved, you can ask about benefits—vacation time, sick leave, medical and dental insurance—if you haven't discussed these already. If you are interviewing at a large company, you may be directed back to the personnel department, whose duty it is to handle such matters. In a smaller or less formal company, your interviewer will go over the benefits with you.

Make sure you understand what you are told about benefits because they are an important part of your remuneration. If you aren't happy with some aspect of them or feel something should be changed, now is the time to bring the matter up. For example, if you have been working for a number of years and do not want to start your new job with the minimum vacation time, you may want to ask for more days off. Do it now. If you have plans for a vacation or time off that you feel you cannot change, inform your prospective boss now. If you wait until after you have been hired, your boss may feel that you were trying to take advantage of the situation.

Benefits are very much part of the entire "package" you are offered by your employer. Just as with the job itself, you have a right to know what this package entails and whether it satisfies your needs.

Closing the Interview

Most likely, you will not get a job offer during the interview. Even if everything has gone well, your interviewer may have other applicants to see, or may just need a few days to think about it before coming to a decision. It is up to your interviewer to tell you what to expect next. If she doesn't say anything, you have the right to ask. "When can I expect to hear from you?" is a good way to begin the discussion.

Your interviewer may be very specific—"I'm almost finished interviewing everybody and I will be making a decision by the end of the week"—or vague—"I'll make a decision soon." Sometimes you will get a good indication of where you stand: "You're definitely at the top of my list"; "Your qualifications are great." Whatever the answer, the important thing is that you both understand what is to happen next.

If your interviewer seems unwilling to give you many specifics, don't read too much into this and don't press the issue. She has told you what she has told you and the reasons for not being more specific may vary. Pressing too hard will only backfire.

Once you have come to an understanding of what the next stage in the process will be, prepare to leave. Thank your interviewer for seeing you, and follow her lead as she escorts you either out of the office or back to personnel. As you leave, again, try to notice your surroundings. Although you may be tired, you are probably more relaxed and will be more apt to notice things. If you see something about the office that seems worth discussing, save it and bring it up if you are officially offered the job.

Reviewing the Interview

Once you have left the premises where your interview has taken place, find a quiet place and spend fifteen or twenty minutes evaluating what you have just been through. Once again your little notebook will come in handy to jot down your thoughts and ideas before you forget them.

In evaluating your interview, first of all, it is important not to personalize it. If your interviewer hasn't seemed overly enthusiastic, it is always tempting to write the interview off. "Oh, if she would have liked me, she would have spent more time with me." "If he was really interested, he would have asked me more questions." As stated many times before, the reasons for an interviewer's behavior can vary a great deal. Don't try to figure out why your interviewer behaved one way or another. You will just be wasting your time.

And don't waste time agonizing over the outcome. There is no way to predict whether you will be offered the job. Time will tell.

What you can do with this time is focus on your own behavior during the interview and see what you can learn from the experience. Ask yourself the following questions:

- Was there anything you did that you are particularly happy or unhappy about? Why? Was it a response to a question or did it have something to do with your general demeanor? What would you say or do differently in the future?

- What did you think of your interviewer's questions? Were there any particular questions that you had never been asked before? Did any of them point out weaknesses that you should review for the future?
- How do you feel about the job you interviewed for? Is there anything you forgot to ask? Make a note to bring it up if you get the job offer.
- How do you feel about the tone of the interview and the direction it took? Was there anything you could have done to make it more favorable to you? Were you an active enough participant?

Sitting down for fifteen or twenty minutes gives you the chance to analyze the specifics of the interview before they all blur in your memory. Rather than worrying about what just took place, look at it as a chance to learn and prepare for your next interview.

The Thank-you Note

"All things being equal, it is the thank-you note that will make a difference. But it can also ruin your chances," said a manager at a clothing manufacturing firm as he relates the following story. He was interviewing people for a sales job and had narrowed down the field to two candidates. A few days after the interviews were finished, he received a note from one of the two finalists, thanking him for seeing her. She also mentioned that she had been in a department store and had bought only clothes manufactured by his firm because they were "the best." The other finalist got the job.

Why? The manager was put off by the cutesy tone of the thank you note, and he did not believe for an instant that the only clothes the woman bought were made by his firm or that she really believed they were the best.

The above anecdote illustrates the biggest peril of thank-you notes. If you try to be cute or gimmicky, you do so at your own risk.

But do send a thank-you note—on the very day you have the interview. Make it short, just one or two sentences, and keep the tone professional and honest. Being cute will only make the note a negative, not a positive. If you think, that during the interview, you forgot to bring up an important point which will reflect well on you, mention it now. But remember, one or two sentences will suffice. Anything longer will seem long-winded.

Thank your interviewer for seeing you and reiterate your desire for the job. The extra effort you take in writing the note will show your interviewer that you really do want the job, and if you are running neck and neck with another candidate, the note may tip the balance in your favor.

About the Author

A free-lance writer, Andrew Ambraziejus is the author of *No Nonsense Management* and *Managing Time*. He lives in New York City.

If you enjoyed this No Nonsense Guide you may want to order these other No Nonsense Guides:

ITEM No.	TITLE	PRICE
0681414049	Managing Time	4.95
0681414030	No Nonsense Management	4.95
0681414952	Successful Interviewing	4.95
0681410477	How To Write a Resume	4.95
0681410450	How To Choose a Career	4.95
0681413891	How to Re-enter The Work Force	4.95

Ordering is easy and convenient.
Order by phone with Visa, MasterCard, American Express or Discover:
☎ **1-800-322-2000,** Dept. 706
or send your order to:
Longmeadow Press, Order/Dept. 706,
P.O. Box 305188, Nashville, TN 37230-5188

Name _____

Address _____

City _____ State _____ Zip _____

Item No.	Title	Qty	Total

Check or Money Order enclosed Payable to Longmeadow Press

Charge: ❑ MasterCard ❑ VISA ❑ American Express ❑ Discover

Account Number

Card Expires

Signaure _____ Date _____

Subtotal	
Tax	
Shipping	2.95
Total	

Please add your applicable sales tax: AK, DE, MT, OR, 0.0%—CO, 3.8%—AL, HI, LA, MI, WY, 4.0%—VA. 4.5%—GA, IA, ID IN, MA, MD, ME, OH, SC, SD, VT, WI, 5.0%—AR, AZ, 5.5%—MO, 5.725%—KS, 5.9%—CT, DC, FL, KY, NC, ND, NE, NJ, PA WV, 6.0%—IL, MN, UT, 6.25%—MN, 6.5%—MS, NV, NY, RI, 7.0%—CA, TX, 7.25%—OK, 7.5%—WA. 7.8%—TN, 8.25%